This edition first published by Parragon Books in 1995

Produced by
Magpie Books Ltd, London

Unit 13–17, Avonbridge Trading Estate
Atlantic Road
Avonmouth
Bristol BS11 9QD

Cover picture and illustrations courtesy of
Peter Newark's Western Americana

ISBN 0-75250-780-X

A copy of the British Library Cataloguing in Publication Data is available from the British Library.

Typeset by Hewer Text Composition Services, Edinburgh
Printed in Singapore by Printlink International Co.

HEROES OF THE WILD WEST
General Custer

Small Town Boy

George Armstrong Custer, the future general, was born on 5 December 1839 at New Rumley in the Mid-Western state of Ohio. It was one of the many settlements scattered across the American continent that had been built by pioneers following the frontier westwards. Custer's great-uncle, Jacob, had founded the small hamlet in 1812. It stood upon a steep rise, overlooking a grand panorama: the green hills of eastern Ohio, rolling away in every direction.

The Custers were agriculturalists of German stock, who had come from Europe in the middle of the eighteenth century in search of a better life. From Pennsylvania, they had moved to Maryland, where Armstrong's father, Emanuel Custer, was born in 1806. Brought up a blacksmith and farmer, like his father before him, Emanuel had journeyed westwards to New Rumley as a young man.

Father Custer was a good-humoured, hearty man with the impressive physique of a frontiersman. He was a staunch Democrat, who enjoyed political discussion and set great store by being a self-made man. He was also a firm Methodist with strong views on the sinfulness of liquor drinking, tobacco smoking and gambling, and had helped to found the small Methodist church in the village.

In 1828 he married his first wife, but she died six years afterwards, leaving three children. Three years later he married Maria Ward Kilpatrick, a young widow living in New Rumley with children of her own.

The first two children of their union died in infancy, but the third was stronger and survived. George Armstrong, nicknamed Autie, enjoyed a unique position in the established family. When he was only about four years old, his proud father began taking him to the drill meetings of the local militia – the New Rumley Invincibles. Clad in a velvet suit with bold brave buttons, Autie would march after the men as fast as his legs would carry him.

Meanwhile, the Custer family was increasing, with three young brothers and a sister for Autie in the next eleven years. With the children from the first marriages as well, the house was always full of noise. Emanuel roused his sons with loud 'hallos' and loved playing practical jokes – a taste which Autie shared to the full.

After the age of ten Autie was sent to the Stebbins Academy in Monroe, Michigan, where he stayed with his married half-sister, Anne Reed. Monroe was a quiet country town on the shores of Lake Erie, named in honour of a presidential visit of 1817. Although the population only numbered some 3,500, it was cosmopolitan compared to New Rumley. For the first time Autie felt conscious of his small-town origins.

The Stebbins Academy offered the best education then available in the Mid-West. Although elementary education in America had been established at public expense, secondary and advanced education were still private. Emanuel Custer paid for his son's schooling out of the savings from their small farm, and Autie returned to help him with his farm work every holiday.

Autie seems to have been happy at the Stebbins Academy. A great wrestler and runner, he was more interested in sport than study, but he was bright and did well at his lessons. At the age of fourteen he moved to the local seminary. He was already considering a military career and would have liked to go to the West Point Military Academy but lacked the backing and the means to do so.

His second choice was a career in education, and after obtaining his teacher's certificate, he began teaching at the small village school of Beech Point. His habit of starting every lesson by playing the accordion made him especially popular with his pupils.

While he was at Beech Point School, Autie fell in love with Mary Holland, the daughter of his landlord. He besieged her with letters and poems, pressing her to marry him. Her father objected, however, and it was perhaps with the intention of ridding himself of his daughter's exuberant suitor that he began to pull the strings to find him a place at West Point. John Wirt, another leading figure in the area, may also have made approaches on Custer's behalf.

Encouraged by their support, Custer sought the help of their local Congressman, John Bingham, and in 1857, at the age of seventeen, he set off for the United States Military Academy at West Point. The decision to go there had been discussed with all his family, and his parents had given him their consent. Indeed, to raise the money for his son's outfitting, Emanuel Custer had sold the small farm.

West Point

Established by Thomas Jefferson in 1802 as a military school for young gentlemen, West Point stands on the west bank of the Hudson River, some 50 miles north of New York. Encircled by mountains, it occupies a plateau about 180 feet above the river, reached by a roadway cut into the cliff.

The Corps of Cadets consisted of one cadet from each congressional district (appointed on recommendation by members of Congress). In the summer of 1857, 108 boys took the entrance examination: 68 passed, among them George Armstrong Custer. Ahead lay a prison-like existence. The cadets could expect to be drummed awake, drummed to meals and drummed to bed, with only arithmetic for diversion. Drills and dress parades would be held all year round and the summer months would be devoted to encampments. They would rise at dawn, turn out for parade, and toil with mathematics, tactics and French before

George Armstrong Custer as
a West Point cadet.

Custer's cavalry brigade in battle near Culpeper, Virginia.

breakfast, followed by more memorization, recitations and dress parades. Not for nothing has West Point been described as one of the 'most absolute despotisms on earth'. But the cadets endured and shared the hardships in the knowledge that they would eventually be counted among America's elite.

Custer wrote that his career as a cadet had but little to commend it to the study of those who came after him, unless as an example to be carefully avoided. If it was not the illegal stewpan hidden up his chimney, it was his disorderly uniform, his unpolished shoes, his slackness in drill, his talking on parade and gambling in quarters that made him the despair of his superior officers. He spent many Saturdays in punishment, performing extra tours of guard duty. However, he was careful not to drop out of the course. He was much given to pranks. Once when asked to translate *Leopold, duc d'autriche* ('Duke of Austria') in a French lesson, he began, 'Leopold, duck and ostrich'.

Meanwhile, another chapter of history was about to unfold as America moved slowly towards Civil War between the northern and southern states. It would begin with the bombardment of Fort Sumter on 12 April 1861 and come to an end, in April 1865, with the surrender of the South.

By the autumn of 1860, the approaching struggle was the usual subject of conversation among the West Point cadets. They followed the debate as North and South argued passionately over economic policies, the slavery problem and the issue of state rights versus loyalty to the Union. When Abraham Lincoln won the presidential elections, South Carolina formally withdrew from the Union. By February 1861, Georgia and seven other southern states had gone the same way. Eventually eleven of them formed the Confederate States of America. Jefferson Davis was chosen president of this confederacy, and his government prepared to repel the expected attack of the northern states.

The places at West Point occupied by cadets from the South became vacant one by one. Best friends would meet on opposite sides during the conflict. Custer did not want to fight his southern classmates, but he wanted the Union kept together, therefore he would fight on the side of the North. Yet before that happened, he was arrested and courtmartialled on a charge of failing to stop a fist-fight between two cadets while officer of the guard. He watched from the guardhouse as members of his class received their marching orders for Washington for the opening chapter of the war.

Through Trials to Triumph

In Washington, Custer's classmates interceded on his behalf and the proceedings of his court-martial were deferred. Released from his arrest, he hurried to the capital, only delaying a few hours in New York to purchase his lieutenant's outfit of sabre, revolver, sash and spurs at the military firm of Horstmanns.

As second lieutenant assigned to the Second Cavalry, Custer reached Bull Run, Virginia, on the morning of the first great battle of the war, 21 July 1861. Commanding the opposing forces were two former West Point classmates, Generals McDowell and Beauregard. McDowell had orders to advance on and capture Richmond, the Confederate capital. Presently, Custer heard the vicious sound of cannon shot as it whirled through the air, then watched in dismay as the tide of the battle turned. The Union troops, not yet disciplined to bear the strain of battle, broke and fled in confusion. Custer's unit was one of the last to leave the battlefield, and he was later cited for bravery. Fortunately, the equally raw Confederates had been in no condition to pursue.

Stung by the humiliation of Bull Run, the North determined to crush the rebellion of the South at all costs. A new general, McClellan, was brought in to organize and train the famous Army of the Potomac. The fighting would start in deadly earnest the next year. Nearly 600,000 men would serve the Union against 350,000 Confederates. Meanwhile, officers from West Point were in great demand for staff duty. Custer served briefly as an aide to Brigadier-General Kearny.

General Custer during the Civil War.

Elizabeth (Libbie) Custer.

Kearny, who had lost an arm leading a cavalry charge in the Mexican war, was one of those model soldiers who was always to be found where the danger was greatest. He taught the young lieutenant much about military discipline. Custer served in the defence movements around Washington until October when he returned to Monroe.

Returning to his post in February 1862 – now with the Fifth Cavalry – Custer was immediately ordered aloft in a balloon (a device used by the Federals at the beginning of the war for watching enemy movements). His quick observations, accurate memory and proficiency in map drawing were invaluable. In his spare time he grabbed at every chance to get into action. His letters home described his adventures, how 'everyone got behind a tree and blazed away as hard as he could'. Custer's daring and energy, and, in particular, a spirited reconnaissance on the Chickahominy River, brought him to the notice of McClellan himself. The lieutenant could not believe his good fortune when McClellan asked him onto his staff with the rank of captain. Like most of the Army of the Potomac he worshipped the general. For his part, McClellan liked the reckless boy, who seemed undeterred by fatigue, and unconscious of fear.

Custer served McClellan faithfully until the general was relieved of his command in the autumn. By now the second Union advance on Richmond had ended in failure. The fall of McClellan meant the end of Custer's captaincy and he returned to Monroe to await further orders.

At a Thanksgiving party that winter Captain Custer was formally presented to his future wife, Elizabeth Bacon. Slender and attractive, with chestnut hair and a pretty oval face,

Libbie was the only surviving child of Judge Daniel Bacon, a prominent figure in Monroe. Elizabeth well remembered their first meeting. Custer, though shy and reticent, had seemed simple and direct. They exchanged only a few words, but the next day, as she was going to her dressmakers, she saw Custer coming down the street. After she rang the bell, she turned and saw him looking at her. They had only met once, but how pleased she was! It was not long before they were seeing each other almost every day.

The pleasures of Monroe society and his courtship of Libbie had to be abandoned in the spring of 1863 when Custer was called back to the front. By now Judge Bacon had heard the gossip circulating around Monroe and had forbidden Libbie to see her dashing captain, being opposed to a military life for his only daughter. Nevertheless, Custer persevered, and Libbie arranged for them to correspond secretly through a mutual friend.

The winter of 1862–3 was a period of gloom for the North, especially after the third attempt to take Richmond, under Burnside (McClellan's successor), had ended in disaster at the battle of Fredericksburg. Burnside was replaced by General Hooker, known as 'Fighting Joe', who proceeded to reorganize the Army of the Potomac energetically. In particular, he gave the cavalry a more important role than its original one of acting chiefly as a screen for infantry. The head of Hooker's newly formed cavalry corps was Brigadier-General Pleasonton, to whom Custer now reported for duty.

Pleasonton liked his energetic young aide, seeing in him the makings of a cavalry leader. Within a few weeks he had recommended him for promotion to the rank of brigadier-general of volunteers for his gallant

General Sheridan in conference with his officers.

The Movement West, Mort Kunstler.

conduct at the battle of Aldie, and organized for him a brigade of Michigan regiments. At twenty-three Custer was the youngest general in the Union army. A conspicuous character since the beginning of the war, he now surpassed himself. He wore a uniform of black velveteen lavishly trimmed in gold lace. There was a brilliant scarlet cravat around his neck, and on his head a soft, wide-brimmed Confederate hat that he had picked up on the field. His hair was long and in curls almost to his shoulders. One officer described him as 'one of the funniest looking beings you ever saw . . . like a circus rider gone mad!'

Custer distinguished himself at the head of the Michigan cavalry brigade in the battle of Gettysburg in July 1863 and frequently did good service in the remaining operations of the campaign of 1863. He was the very model of a light cavalry officer, wrote a contemporary, 'quick in observation, clear in judgement and resolute and determined in execution'. His men boasted: 'Our boy general never says "Go in, men!" He says, "Come on, boys!" and in we go, you bet.'

Wounded at the battle of Culpepper in October 1863, Custer returned to Monroe, where he was greeted as something of a hero. In a short time, he and Libbie secretly became engaged. After a preliminary resistance the Judge gave his consent to the marriage and even went to call on Custer's father. Libbie reported that the meeting had gone well: Emanuel had assured her father that she was getting the 'best of boys for a husband'. The wedding took place on 9 February 1864.

Meanwhile, Virginia was destined to be the scene of some of the bitterest fighting of the whole war. At last Lincoln had found a commander-in-chief, General Ulysses S. Grant, who could match up to the brilliant

Confederate general, Robert E. Lee. Grant's singleness of purpose and driving energy were the qualities necessary to check Lee and finally subdue the Confederacy. He brought in General Sheridan, who replaced Pleasonton as cavalry chief in the spring of 1864. After meeting Sheridan, Custer informed Libbie that the Major-General had impressed him very favourably.

The honeymoon had been cut short at the end of February, when Custer had been ordered back to the front. Libbie went with her husband to his cavalry headquarters at Stevensburg, Virginia, within view of enemy pickets. Of the many sights that impressed her, not least was that of her husband's cook, Eliza, calmly making supper under fire. Eliza was a runaway slave who had decided to free herself after the Emancipation Proclamation of January 1863. Since the beginning of the war many slaves had escaped their southern masters and gone to work in Union camps. From Stevensburg, Libbie retired to the safety of a boarding house in Washington where she anxiously awaited news of her husband. With her charm, she was a welcome guest at social gatherings, where she met influential congressmen, even President Lincoln, who teased her: 'So this is the young woman whose husband goes into a charge with a whoop and a shout.'

Meanwhile, long trains of ambulances were trailing through Washington and the lists of the dead and wounded were growing ever longer. At the beginning of May, Grant pressed towards Richmond, meeting with stiff resistance from the skilful Lee. A forested area called the Wilderness was set ablaze by cannonfire in a two-day battle that resulted in staggering losses for both sides. Yet, unlike previous Union generals, Grant refused to retreat. Through many weary months, he kept hammering at Lee's defences, pushing him back to the lines of Richmond and Petersburg. Then, in a famous episode of the war, the aggressive Sheridan chased the Confederate General Early out of the Shenandoah valley and laid it waste.

Under Sheridan, Custer took part in the various actions of the cavalry in the Wilderness and Shenandoah campaigns. Promoted to the position of commander of the Third Division of the cavalry corps, he left his loyal Michigan cavalry brigade behind at the end of September 1864. (Over 400 men petitioned to be transferred with him, but were refused.) Custer went on to win further military honours with the Third Division. At the battle of Woodstock he came face to face with a former West Point classmate, General Thomas Rosser, now commanding the Confederate cavalry. Custer rode to the front of the line and saluted Rosser, then swiftly moved his men into a charge, driving the unprepared enemy back for some twenty-six miles. Soon afterwards Custer was made major-general. His madcap younger brother Tom had risen through the ranks in the meantime, and now served under him. They spent Christmas together with Libbie and other friends and relatives at army headquarters in Winchester.

It was in the pursuit of Lee's army from Richmond in the spring of 1865 that Custer won his greatest glory. Day and night, with little pause for rest and food, his division had kept striking relentlessly at the line of retreat. It was to Custer that a Confederate flag of truce was brought with the news that General Lee had gone to meet Grant to discuss the future of the armies. Custer was present at Appomattox Court House to see Lee surrender to Grant on the afternoon of Palm Sunday, 9 April 1865. Afterwards, as a present for his wife, Sheridan gave him the small table on which Grant had written the terms of surrender. 'I know of no one', wrote Sheridan to Libbie, whose efforts had 'contributed more to bring about this desirable result than your gallant husband.'

US Cavalry fighting Indians, by Charles Schreyvogel.

Sioux Indian hunting Buffalo, school of George Catlin.

Life on the Plains

Custer's career during the war had been a brilliant one. He had had eleven horses shot under him and had achieved the rank of general when only twenty-three. He enjoyed one final triumph at the Washington Grand Parade on 23 May 1865, when his horse bolted and galloped down the avenue past the crowds and the President's stand. By a magnificent exhibition of horsemanship, he conquered the runaway steed. The *Detroit Evening News* described him as the 'brave, yellow-haired chief'.

After the war, Custer was sent to Texas for duty under Sheridan. By late June 1865 he had arrived at Alexandria, Louisiana, having taken a steamboat from New Orleans up the Red River under soft southern skies, past orange groves and red clay river banks that were home to alligators sunning themselves. At Alexandria he took command of a division of cavalry which he had orders to march to Hempstead in Texas.

For the first time Custer encountered problems of discipline. The war had given him an exalted view of his leadership abilities, for now it was only by applying harsh discipline that he was able to manage the threatening faces around him. The men, who belonged to volunteer regiments from the Mid-West, wanted to go home now the war was over, not to Texas. Many were deserting or pilfering from the local population. They hated Custer, who seemed to have all the egotism and self-importance typical of a young man. With Sheridan's approval, Custer resorted to severe punishments, such as twenty-five lashes and head-shaving. He even executed one deserter.

On 8 August the division marched out of Alexandria at the beginning of the 150-mile trek westwards to Hempstead, Texas. The march took nineteen days in great heat. Custer showed his usual powers of endurance, trotting off on his own at the end of the day while all his men were resting. They made camp near Hempstead, and then, in November, moved on to Austin, the state capital. Remarkably, Mrs Custer accompanied the soldiers on the march.

Custer remained in Texas until the

Portrait of Custer in his buckskins,
by H.H. Cross.

Custer and Scouts during the Yellowstone expedition of 1873.

beginning of 1866, when the army was reorganised and he lost his honorary rank of major-general. He returned to Monroe in the spring and left for the East soon afterwards to seek new opportunities, either business, political or military. Clearly, he was most suited for a military career. On 28 July the organization of the Seventh Cavalry was authorized, and Custer was assigned to it with the rank of lieutenant-colonel.

In October the Custers went west to Fort Riley, Kansas, where the Seventh Cavalry had its headquarters. Fort Riley stood on a wide plateau at the junction of the Republican and Smoky Hill rivers. It was the sort of isolated spot where boredom is a major problem. Most of the Seventh were hard drinkers. Custer, though a teetotaller and non-smoker, who seldom swore, had a reputation as a gambler and 'habitué of demi-monde dives'. It seems that the Seventh was not a happy regiment. In part this may have been because the varied backgrounds of the enlisted men and their diverse motives for selecting army life led to a lack of cohesion and *esprit de corps*. But it is also likely that some fault lay in Custer's own character. He clearly alienated a number of the officers. Major Reno concealed any animosity he may have felt; but Virginian-born Captain Benteen came away from his first meeting with the general complaining that he had heard 'no such bragging as was stuffed into me on that night'.

Ever since the discovery of gold in California in 1848, the vast region of *terra incognita* beyond the Mississippi had lured thousands of White settlers westwards. Shrinking from their approach were the native Indians, Sioux, Pawnee and Cheyenne, whose way of life depended on hunting the roaming buffalo herds of the Great Plains. They fought desperately to defend their ancient hunting grounds from the White man who was stealing their land and from the threatening transcontinental railroads which were being built across the Plains. It was natural that the army should be sent to the West to protect the settlers and make the building of railroads, wagon roads and telegraphs possible

Custer knew nothing about the Indians or Indian fighting when he led the Seventh on their first Indian campaign under General Hancock in the spring of 1867. His first encounter was at the Indian village of Roman Nose at Pawnee Fork, where a line of Indians in battle order met to parlay with Hancock's forces. Dressed in their brightest colours, their heads crowned with the brilliant war-bonnet, their lances bearing the crimson pennant, bows strung and quivers full of barbed arrows, they made a formidable sight. It was agreed that talks should be resumed the next morning, but despite their brave show, the Indians had no wish for a further confrontation and abandoned the village during the night. After sending Custer with the Seventh in pursuit, Hancock moved his infantry into the deserted camp and systematically destroyed it.

When news of the burning reached the Indians, they took to the war path, raiding stage stations and attacking railroad workers' camps in revenge. Meanwhile, Custer searched for them high and low, but failed to catch anyone. Or anything, for it was on the march that he had his first buffalo adventure. Galloping ahead of his men, he found a very large buffalo and started chasing it. He flew after the animal for mile after mile until at last he decided to shoot it. And then he shot his horse instead of the buffalo! It had been far from wise to desert his marching column in the midst of enemy territory. Only by a stupen-dous stroke of luck was he eventually

Chief Sitting Bull

Custer in the Library at
Fort Abraham Lincoln.

found by his surprised command. Shortly afterwards they made camp at Fort Hays.

Before the summer was over, the first Indian campaign ended even more ignominiously for 'Hard Backsides' Custer. While scouting the country, the Seventh had been involved in a number of unpleasant incidents: an Indian attack on a wagon train that Custer unwisely sent to Fort Wallace for supplies (and to pick up his wife if she had been there); the massacre of one of the young lieutenants and his party; and the desertion of nearly forty men in one night, caused by the regiment marching too close to a road leading to the Colorado gold mines. When another thirty men deserted the next day, Custer ruthlessly ordered a chase to bring 'none in alive'. According to Benteen the dismounted deserters were shot down while begging for their lives.

When the Seventh came to Fort Wallace on 13 July, Custer's usually buoyant spirits were low. It seems that he received an anonymous letter telling him to 'hustle back and look out for family interest'. Libbie was over 150 miles away at Fort Riley. Recklessly, Custer decided to go and visit her. Assembling four officers and seventy-two troopers, he force-marched them across Kansas to the point of exhausting both horses and men. A few stragglers from the column were waylaid by Indians. When they reached Fort Hays, Custer pushed on to Fort Harker, then took the train to Fort Riley. His motives were clear. Libbie awoke to hear the clank of a sabre and the quick, springing steps of feet. There before her stood her husband.

The dash across Kansas led to Custer's courtmartial and suspension from rank and pay for a year, on charges of deliberate absence from duty and mistreatment of captured deserters. A number of the officers of the Seventh breathed a sigh of relief. If Custer ever came back they hoped he would show more sense and judgement than on his first tour.

The Custers spent the winter quietly at Fort Leavenworth, where Armstrong began writing his Civil War memoirs. Later they returned to Monroe for the summer. In the autumn of 1868, Custer was restored to active duty in Kansas for a winter campaign against the Plains Indians. He arrived with his hair cut short and a perfect menagerie of Scotch foxhounds.

On 27 November 1868, Custer led the Seventh Cavalry in a dawn attack on an Indian village, established by the Cheyenne chief Black Kettle, a champion of peace, in the valley of the Washita River. Only the day before, Black Kettle had returned from a journey to Fort Cobb to convince the commander of the fort of his peaceful intentions. Yet Sheridan had ordered Custer to destroy the Indian villages and ponies; to shoot or hang all warriors and bring back all women and children. Within minutes the deed was done; in another few minutes, the troopers had shot nearly 700 Indian ponies. They had killed 103 Cheyennes of all ages and both sexes (among them Black Kettle) and taken prisoner women and children.

Custer was lucky to escape with a victory before Indian reinforcements from a number of other villages, spread widely along the valley, started to appear on the bluffs surrounding his position. In the retreat, he failed to look for one of his officers and nineteen men who had gone missing. Later he would be severely criticized for having left the officer and his party to their fate: Indians had surrounded them and had killed every one.

Although there was a feeling among the older officers of the Seventh and among many Americans that Custer should not have attacked Black

Detail from *Custer's Last Stand*, E.S. Paxson.

CUSTER KILLED.

DISASTROUS DEFEAT OF THE AMERICAN TROOPS BY THE INDIANS.

SLAUGHTER OF OUR BEST AND BRAVEST.

GRANT'S INDIAN POLICY COME TO FRUIT.

A WHOLE FAMILY OF HEROES SWEPT AWAY.

THREE HUNDRED AND FIFTEEN AMERICAN SOLDIERS KILLED AND THIRTY-ONE WOUNDED.

SALT LAKE, U. T., July 5.—The correspondent of the Helena (Mon.) *Herald* writes from Still water, Mon., under date of July 2, as follows:

Muggins Taylor, a scout for General Gibbon, arrived here last night direct from Little Horn River and reports that General Custer found the Indian camp of 2,000 lodges on the Little Horn and immediately attacked it.

He charged the thickest portion of the camp with five companies. Nothing is k[illegible]n of the operations of this detachment, except their course as traced by the dead. Major Reno commanded the other seven companies and attacked the lower portion of the camp.

Report of the Little Bighorn battle in *New York World*.

Kettle's peaceful village, the Washita established Custer's reputation and that of the Seventh as the nation's foremost Indian fighters. When they came back into camp on 2 December, Sheridan ordered the entire post out for a formal review. They marched past with sabres flashing and the band playing. As at the end of the Civil War, Sheridan congratulated Custer for 'efficient and gallant services rendered'.

The Last Battle

The Custers remained in Kansas for the next two years, camping on Big Creek, near Fort Hays, in the summers of 1869 and 1870, and residing at Fort Leavenworth during the winter of 1869–70. Much of their time was spent entertaining congressmen and other visitors from the east coast who wanted to be shown the romantic country and the buffalo herds before they disappeared. Custer looked the very picture of a great plainsman in his heavily fringed buckskin suit.

Being ordered south to the small settlement of Elizabethtown, Kentucky, in 1871 was a blow to any hopes Custer may have had of promotion. Elizabethtown was a dreary place and Custer's chief duty was in suppressing the local Ku Klux Klan, the secret society formed in the Southern states after the Civil War to oppose the rights of former slaves. His ample spare time was spent reading and writing. Out of the Kentucky interlude came article after article written for the *Galaxy* magazine about his experiences in Kansas. The twenty instalments were later published in book form as *My Life on the Plains*. He was becoming a literary lion.

Just as life was becoming monotonous, Custer was summoned to take the Grand Duke Alexis of Russia (third son of Alexander II) on a buffalo hunt. Having purchased Alaska from Russia in 1867, the American government wanted to show its good will. The hunt was a spectacular Wild West show. Besides Custer, the party included Buffalo Bill Cody (the most famous of all

The horse Comanche, sole survivor of Custer's division.

Poster for the 1967 film of Custer's life.

hunters) and a band of 'friendly' Sioux Indians. Delighted with the hunting and with the fun-loving Custer, Alexis insisted that he (later joined by Libbie) accompany him for the rest of his tour. The holiday ended in March 1872 at New Orleans, where Alexis took ship for Russia.

In 1873 Custer was transferred to the northern plains of Dakota, where he would remain for the last few years of his life. The Seventh was reunited at Memphis, then proceeded to Fort Rice, Dakota Territory. Their assignment was to protect the surveyors of the Northern Pacific

Railroad, who were extending it across Sioux territory, following the Yellowstone River. The expedition started from Fort Rice on 20 June 1873. It consisted of twenty companies of infantry, ten of cavalry (under Custer), Indian scouts, the Northern Pacific engineers, a large wagon train and a herd of beef cattle. In overall command was Major-General Stanley, a quiet, competent but often drunken soldier, who clashed with Custer almost at once. Custer disliked Stanley's drinking and Stanley found Custer's habit of charging on ahead insufferable. In no time Stanley had Custer arrested and relegated to the rear of the column, although two days later he apologized and lifted the arrest.

Custer might have been made of India rubber. He was in transports of delight at the sublime scenery of the Yellowstone valley and the magnificent hunting, with antelope, elk, deer and buffalo. He collected crates full of fossils and examined the flora and fauna with enthusiasm. He wrote epic letters to Libbie embellishing his accomplishments. To add to the enjoyment he had met up with his old West Point friend and opponent in the Civil War, Thomas Rosser, now chief engineer of the survey. In the evenings they stretched out on a buffalo robe under the fly of the tent, exchanging war stories in the moonlight.

The Seventh returned from the Yellowstone expedition even more famous for its success against the Indians and its exploratory achievements. They had handled several skirmishes with Sioux warriors admirably and helped the surveyors prepare for the next phase of building the Northern Pacific railroad. Next, Custer took command of Fort Abraham Lincoln, on flat land across the river from Bismarck, where the Northern Pacific railroad stopped.

Descriptions of life at Fort Lincoln are of a gay and lively scene. Custer's kennels at the back of the house were full of the finest breeds of fox and stag hounds, and his stable contained his favourite thoroughbreds, Dandy and Vic. There was a large Custer faction at the fort: his brothers Tom and Boston, who had a commissary post, Calhoun, his brother-in-law, and Captain Yates from Monroe. The officers often gathered on the porch in front of Custer's house to chat and smoke. The evenings were spent in singing, piano playing and parlour games of all kinds. Often Custer would hide himself in his library, which was decorated with furs and skins, grand heads of buffalo and hunting trophies. He spent hours improving himself, reading Napier's *Peninsular* or writing.

In the summer of 1874 the government authorized an expedition to the Black Hills, a ridge of pine-dark peaks and high blue lakes rising out of the plains of Dakota, which had been reserved to the Sioux nation in the Fort Laramie treaty of 1868. Of all their domain the Indians perhaps loved the Black Hills the best. They named them *He Sapa* or black because of their colour, and regarded them as sacred. The purpose of the government expedition was firstly to establish a military post in the heart of Indian country, and secondly, to investigate the possibility of gold. Under Custer's command, the expedition set out from Fort Abraham Lincoln on 2 July 1874.

Already alarmed by the crews who were building the Northern Pacific Railroad, the Indians watched in dismay as 'Long Hair' Custer with his blue-uniformed horsemen and canvas-covered supply wagons invaded their sanctuary. After Custer reported that the rumours of gold were true, thousands of unemployed prospectors poured into the hills along the tracks left by his supply wagons. The Indians called the trail the Thieves Road, and Custer the 'chief of all thieves'. The Sioux War would begin a year and a half later when, despite previous treaties, the government decided that the Sioux should give up their claims to the Black Hills and move to a reservation by 31 January 1876. They refused.

Custer was to have commanded the expedition ordered to set out early in 1876 to help round up the hostile Sioux and Cheyenne, especially the bands under the celebrated chiefs Sitting Bull and Crazy Horse. In the middle of March, however, he was ordered to Washington to testify before a congressional committee regarding frauds in the Indian service. His testimony, unfavourable to Belknap, the former Secretary of War, offended President Grant: he not only deprived Custer of his command, substituting Terry, the district commander, but ordered that he should not even be permitted to accompany the expedition. However, a storm of popular disapproval, joined with the earnest plea of Terry, caused Grant to relent. Custer was restored to command of the Seventh under the supervision of Terry.

On May 17 General Terry's expedition of approximately 1,000 men left

Fort Abraham Lincoln and marched westwards to the Powder River, eventually making camp some twenty miles south of its confluence with the Yellowstone on the evening of June 7. A few weeks later, on June 22, Custer broke away from the main command with orders to move up the Rosebud Creek in pursuit of an impresssive Indian trail. Terry chose a different route, intending to block a possible Indian escape.

The Seventh Cavalry now began the arduous march over rough and tortuous country that would end tragically at the Little Bighorn. Two factors contributing to the defeat would be the weariness of the men before they entered battle and the fact that roughly a quarter of the regiment were new recruits unfamiliar with battle. By June 24 they knew that the Indian camp was nearby. Custer ordered a night march to the divide between the Little Bighorn River and Rosebud Creek. In the early hours of the next day, at a place called Crow's Nest, scouts spied a large Indian encampment stretched along the west bank of the Little Bighorn River. It was decided they should attack immediately.

Though no one knew exactly at the time, the camp consisted of circle after circle of tepees – of the Oglala under Crazy Horse and the Hunkpapa under Sitting Bull, aswell as the Cheyenne, Arapaho, bands of Minnecojou and a number of Blackfeet and Sans Arc. Their number has been estimated between 3,000 and 7,000 people, with from 800 to 2,000 warriors, far outweighing the strength of Custer's Seventh Cavalry – in all about 600 men.

For the Indians it had been a glorious last summer away from the government reservations, hunting and feasting and dancing as of old. At a great sun dance, held at Medicine Rocks in the second week of June, Sitting Bull had had a vision in which he saw soldiers, falling like grasshoppers with their heads down and their hats falling off. They were falling right into the Indian camp.

By about 8.45 am on the morning of Sunday 25 June, the Seventh was on the move. Shortly after noon, Custer divided his force into three battalions. A fourth column, escorting the packtrain, brought up the rear. While Captain Benteen led some 125 men southwestwards to intercept any Indians who might try to get away, Custer instructed his second-in-command, Major Reno, to ride straight into the valley and strike the southern end of the village. He himself took 210 troopers to the right in order to attack further downstream. (With hindsight Benteen blamed Custer for having scattered the regiment into four columns, none of which were within supporting distance of either of the others).

Climbing the high bluffs along the east bank of the Little Bighorn, Custer could see a part of the immense village. A cloud of dust indicated warriors galloping towards Reno and frightened women and children scattering down the stream and up into the hills in confusion. Extra strength was needed to capture the fugitives and Custer decided to recall Benteen. Then he divided his command, sending one battalion galloping down a ravine into the valley, while posting another on a high ridge to cover them.

Meanwhile, Reno's attack had failed; he had killed helpless villagers, but no warriors. The Indians drove him back to the bluffs where he was saved by the timely arrival of Benteen, who had been proceeding northwards to rejoin Custer. According to Benteen, they tried to follow Custer but saw an immense body of Indians coming at them and were forced to withdraw to a defensible position. The siege lasted two days until the Indians suddenly departed on the afternoon of June 26. By then neither Reno or Benteen knew what had happened to Custer.

It seems that Custer's battalion was wiped out as it pursued the Indian squaws and children who were fleeing the camp. Having forced Reno to make a hasty retreat, hundreds of warriors had rushed back down the valley like a hurricane to attack the soldiers who had descended towards the river. Suddenly caught in heavy fire, the troopers panicked and were killed by the warriors as they tried to flee. An Indian witness saw dust whirling on the hill and horses coming out of it with empty saddles. Herding the terrified soldiers like buffalo, the Indians attacked with bows and arrows and firepower. All was confusion from the smoke of the shooting and the dust of the horses. Next the Indians closed in on Custer's command – now only 60 men strong – which was posted on the slight rise, later called Custer Hill. Some of his men had gone on foot to get help but had fallen under the heavy fire. The Indians crept closer to the soldiers on the hill, crawling through the gullies and sagebrush and using the ridges and knolls for cover until they surrounded them.

Eventually moving in with clubs and hatchets, the warriors rapidly killed all the soldiers. In something short of two hours, Custer's entire battalion of 210 men had been wiped out by the Sioux and Cheyenne.

The bodies were found on the morning of 27 June. Custer lay on top of the hill and around him lay his closest comrades, his brothers Tom and young Boston, and not far off, his nephew Armstrong Reed, who had helped to drive the beef herds. The General was not mutilated at all. He had been hit by a bullet in the left temple and in the left side, at or near the heart.

Sitting Bull's vision had come true and Custer's final gamble had failed; but his famous 'Last Stand' at the Little Bighorn has passed into the mythology of the United States. When the steamer bringing the news of his defeat reached Libbie and the other widows at Fort Lincoln, they prepared to go home. Libbie gave most of the household goods to the post trader and shipped her husband's desk and her heirloom china and silver back to Monroe. Custer's favourite horse, Dandy, went to his father, Emanuel. Several months later, Libbie asked for Custer's remains to be buried at West Point. A riderless horse followed as

the funeral cortege wound its way from the chapel to the cemetery north of the post. Mrs Custer devoted the rest of her life to the memory of her husband. She died a few days before her ninety-second birthday in April 1933, and is buried with him at West Point.

FURTHER MINI SERIES
INCLUDE

HEROES OF THE WILD WEST

General Custer
Butch Cassidy and the Sundance Kid
Billy the Kid
Annie Oakley
Buffalo Bill
Geronimo
Wyatt Earp
Doc Holliday
Sitting Bull
Jesse James